Mealtime Memories

by

Janet Barrass

British Library Cataloguing in Publication Data.

A catalogue record for this book is available from the British Library

ISBN 978 0 86071 805 5

A Commissioned Publication Printed by
MOORLEYS
Print, Design & Publishing
info@moorleys.co.uk · www.moorleys.co.uk

Contents

Introduction

Food nostalgia provides us with such vivid, emotional memories of people and places in our past. Sunday tea-times with tinned fruit and Carnation milk or perhaps a slice from a brick of vanilla ice cream eaten while watching on our black and white telly.

This warm, fuzzy feeling creates a reservoir of positive emotions. It is comforting. Faced with an abundance of confusing choices in the modern world, we often pine for the taste of home-made chips with oxtail soup drizzled on top.

Eating is a social act that helps us cement a connection to shared memories of special moments spent together around a table. These childhood memories always seem wholesome even when the food was the not-so-wholesome: Vesta Chow Mein or butterscotch flavoured Angel Delight.

Remembering these meals and moments shared with our loved ones strengthens our feeling of belonging to a social group. The fact that the foods were often processed and packed with preservatives from the 1970s onwards seems to get lost in nostalgic translation. The thing about food is that it speaks to all five senses, especially the powerful memory triggers of smell and taste.

Food is so fundamental to our survival that we are primed to form strong memories about it. This means we tend to eat with our minds as much as our stomachs. Childhood memories triggered by our sense of smell usually stem from our first ten years of life. Brain scans have revealed that olfactory memory cues – those associated with smell – activate the hippocampus and the amygdala. These areas of the brain are linked with memory and emotional reactions.

Humans have a fundamental need to belong, and because nostalgia often centres around personal events involving people they care about, the evocation of nostalgia is one way in which people can obtain a sense of belonging even when the people they are close to are not physically present. Comfort foods remind us of our social ties, which means they may help us feel less lonely when we feel isolated.

This book has developed as a result of Paul and my experience of working with older people, those with mental health conditions and those who are lonely or isolated.

We run a small social enterprise which involves reminiscence using original artefacts, songs, stories and poems with people, many of whom, but not all, have difficulty with their memory. We find that food and mealtime memories are among the most powerful and enduring, often lasting when other memories have faded.

The memories which are brought back by mealtime reminiscence are generally happy ones, linked directly to events and people who were important to the person. It is not so much about the details of a recipe, but about the circumstances of the food and its preparation which are significant to a person. Food may not always have been plentiful or pleasant. However, the people in the memory linger longer than the flavour of the food.

We hope that you find pleasure in dipping into this collection of reminiscences and discover that your own memories are pleasurably re-kindled.

All people who have contributed recipes and memories have kindly agreed for them to be shared in this book.

All quantities, ingredients, timings and temperatures are subject to the vagaries of memory. In other words, we cannot guarantee that every recipe will turn out to be edible if cooked!

Food for thought – a therapist's perspective

Paul Barrass MRCOT

During the four decades in which I worked as an occupational therapist, I used many of the different types of reminiscence with patients, carers and staff. Good reminiscence work can be achieved with both individuals and groups and the topic of Mealtime Memories was a favourite one with all types of people. It cuts across age, race, gender and personal history. What we eat and drink and our memories about it are part of who we are. Be they happy and joyous memories of time spent with family and friends or less happy memories of poor food and poor circumstances.

This book can be used with individuals or in group work to form a bridge of communication between those participating in a therapeutic session. There is nothing in it that is contrived. All the recipes and memories come from an eclectic group of people. It can also be read for pleasure and may trigger memories of our own lives, families, friends and workplace meals.

Now in retirement from the NHS, Janet and I run "All Around the Shire". I assist Janet in delivering mealtime memories sessions. We would be happy to discuss how this could benefit groups and individuals you may know or be working with. The contact details are on the back page.

We have found these sessions to be especially beneficial to people on the journey of dementia, those suffering mental health problems or feeling isolated and lonely. Even in bringing the book together, it has proved an uplifting experience for those contributing, some of whom initially felt that their memories were not worth recording. This capturing and valuing this type of memory increases ideas of self-worth and reinforces a person's identity. Every single person on this planet has a story to tell if people have the time and patience to let them speak and ask the right questions to encourage them. An acknowledgement of them as a person and their memories are valid. It encourages people to use higher mental processing to tell their story and to re-engage with the emotions that those stories provoke. It can be used inter-generationally for people to speak with others in their own family or social circle about things that are important to them.

Whilst compiling this book, Janet and I have re-engaged with many of our own memories of family and friends and the meals we have shared together.

"Ponder well on this point:

The pleasant hours of our life are all
connected by a more or less tangible link,
with some memory of the table."

Charles Pierre Monselet (1825-1888)

Breakfasts

My granny used to share an egg with her sister as a treat for breakfast. She came from a very poor coal mining family in Wales.

Bread was rationed only after the Second World War, (July 1946 to July 1948) so there was usually a bit of bread and "scrape" or dripping available to set you up for the day. Porridge was eaten as a staple. With the advent of advertising in newspapers, magazines and on television, breakfast cereals became widespread during the 1950s and 60s with cornflakes becoming very popular.

Bacon and eggs or the more substantial "full English" breakfast is very personalised and varies by region and family. Ingredients can include sausages, bacon, eggs, mushrooms, tomatoes, beans, black pudding, fried bread, toast or bread and butter or anything that might go in the frying pan. I have found that the dividing factor in any family is whether to use brown sauce or tomato ketchup on the plate. For me, I love HP brown sauce (not Daddies) while my brother would always choose tomato ketchup.

Sausage Splash

I have seen these only in cafes and roadside butty vans in the Midlands.

It involves a sausage cob or sandwich with a splash of tinned tomatoes. Any combination of sausage, bacon or eggs can be treated this way. Delicious.

In County Durham, gravy, curry sauce, beans or mushy peas can be used on a chip butty to make a Chip Butty Splash.

Dips

"Dips are tomatoes cooked in bacon fat to go with bacon rolls. We used to eat more tomatoes than bacon. The tomatoes were cooked with Bisto and gravy browning.

I remember dipping the pan with bread after the meal was finished."

(Florence Ann Robinson)

One of the memories I have from childhood is dipping soldiers into boiled eggs. The buttered toast was cut into slender slices, wide enough to fit into the top of the egg which had its top cut off. There is great debate about whether to slice the top of the egg off with a knife or whether to bash the top with a spoon and pick off the pieces of the shell before slicing the bald egg with a knife. Whichever way the grand opening was achieved, I would then take a soldier and dip it into the (hopefully) runny yolk and bring it to my mouth before the yolk dribbled down my chin.

A little pinch of salt was put onto the side of the tea plate to season the egg and I felt quite grown up being trusted to sprinkle a small amount of salt onto my egg.

Eggcups were fiercely defended and each child used their own, never trusting another sibling with the prized vessel.

Another personal memory is the practice of making "ducks". This involves a bowl of soup and a chunk of break. If you choose to pull the bread into pieces and lay them on top of the soup, they float around until eaten. Hence: "ducks". I have floated my ducks on a soup pond in polite company and, judging by the looks of disapproval, it is something probably best done when eating alone or with close family.

An Ulster Fry

My beautiful mum, Kathleen Mavourneen, spent most of her childhood and until she was married in the fair city of Belfast. She talks of having this meal cooked by her stepmother on a Saturday morning "and that did you all day" so there was no further need to eat again that day. She remembers going back to visit Belfast in the 1970s, ordering an Ulster Fry from a café and saying that it tasted better than when she was a wee girl.

"2 eggs
Sausage
Bacon
Mushrooms

Tomatoes
Soda farls
Potato bread

Fried in one pan in dripping.

Drizzled in brown sauce (HP of course) and washed down with mugs of tea."

(Kathleen Mavourneen Sharpe)

The contents of an Ulster Fry are hotly debated but several features are key:

Firstly, it needs to be cooked all in the same pan where the flavours mingle together thanks to the generous helpings of lard or dripping, bacon fat and juices from the sausages. These are important to enable the soda and potato bread to absorb the flavours and cook without burning. My mum has identified that there was some sort of "mince and vegetable sausage" involved in the final presentation, but I think this is either leftover mince from a previous meal or black and white sausage.

Next, the breads make this dish unique to the region. Using the ingredients of flour, salt, buttermilk and bicarbonate of soda, soda farls are quicker to make than traditional yeasted bread. Its inclusion in the Ulster Fry has helped the soda farl (which literally means fourths) attain near-legendary status in Northern Ireland. The farl is sliced cross-ways with its cut side facing down into the pan and fried until crisp and golden.

Another delicious ingredient in the Ulster Fry is potato bread, which is made with cooked potatoes, flour, baking powder and buttermilk and also traditionally cut into quarters and cooked on a griddle. It should be golden and crisp on the outside and soft and fluffy in the inside.

Porridge

Use one container of oats to two and a quarter of milk and water with a pinch of salt. Cook, stirring frequently until ready (about 4-5 minutes).

Oats or oatmeal come in a variety of sizes and may or may not be soaked overnight in water before cooking. Irish oatmeal is made when the oat grain kernel is cut into two or three pieces using a steel or metal blade. Scots traditionally stone-grind oats making the pieces of oat smaller and giving a creamier texture to the porridge than Irish oats. Rolled oats (sometimes called old fashioned oats) are created when oat grain kernels are steamed and then rolled into flakes. This process stabilizes the healthy oils in the oats, so they stay fresh longer, and helps the oats cook faster, by creating a greater surface area. If you roll the oat flakes thinner, and/or steam them longer, you create quick oats and ultimately instant oats. The nutrition stays the same (these are all whole grains) but the texture changes.

Traditionally, porridge is stirred with a wooden rod called a 'Spirtle' or 'Spurtle', which looks a bit like a drumstick (not the chicken variety!).

Superstition has it that Scottish porridge should always be stirred clockwise - and preferably with your right hand - otherwise the Devil will come for the person doing the stirring!

Porridge is traditionally served in wooden bowls, and eaten standing up. Each spoonful should be dipped in a bowl of cream that's shared by everyone at the table.

Centuries ago, an authentic porridge recipe such as this one would be used to cook up a big pot and what wasn't eaten for breakfast would be poured into 'drawers' or another container and allowed to cool. Once it was cooled, the porridge could be cut up into slices or blocks, wrapped, and taken along on the days' work to be eaten for lunch, dinner or a snack!

When I was a child, I was told real Scots didn't put anything on their porridge except salt. And if you added cream or sugar, you were soft… or English!

Family and Everyday Meals

Family meals in the 20th century have evolved according to availability of ingredients, cooking equipment and time to prepare and serve it. They have also been influenced by TV and advertising, the rise of cookery programmes beginning with Fanny Craddock in 1955 and Philip Harben from 1956.

The recipes that tend to be fondly remembered, however, involve family sitting around a table. Perhaps people who are no longer with us. Our memorable food does not have to be fancy or "prinked and pranked" but it is usually tasty, cheap and enjoyed by all generations.

Paul's Family Crispy

"1 chopped onion
3 slices bread made into crumbs
1 or 2 rolls of sausage meat
2 eggs
Mixed herbs
A dash of Lea and Perrins Worcestershire sauce
A pinch of pepper

Mix pork and onion in a bowl.

Add eggs and the rest of the ingredients.

Place into a long ceramic dish or metal baking dish.

Rough up the surface so it is nobbly.

Cook on gas 5 for about 1 hour until the top is crispy.

Before serving pull a bit off to taste.

This recipe has been used in my family for over 100 years as our "extra" or alternative stuffing for Christmas day. It is not introduced into a turkey's bottom but cooked separately.

My mum and mum's mum made their own versions of this and, for the last 15 years, I have been making it on Christmas day. It is as good cold for tea as it is hot.

In recent years the Christmas lunch I have cooked is:
Chicken breasts in white wine
Pigs in blankets (sausage with bacon wrapped around)
Crispy
Roast potatoes and parsnips
Carrots, peas
Gravy, redcurrant jelly and bread sauce
Home-made Christmas pud

In the past mum served pineapple as a starter and we sometimes had mince tarts and a cheeseboard as extra courses.

The meal would normally start at 12pm after church or a trip to the cemetery in more recent years to place a wreath on dad's grave."

(Paul Barrass)

Tuna Plait

"8oz plain flour
Pinch salt
2oz lard
2oz margarine
3 or more oz grated cheese
2 tbsp cold water
7oz tuna
1 small onion finely chopped
Squeeze of lemon juice
A little beaten egg

Make shortcrust pastry with the flour, fats and 1oz of the cheese.

Mix together tuna, onion, lemon juice and the rest of the cheese.

Roll out the pastry into a rectangle about 8 inches long and dampen the edges.

Pile the filling down the centre of the pastry. Make slits either side of the filling at one- inch intervals and cross these alternately over the filling to form a plait.

Seal to and bottom and brush with egg.

Bake in hot oven for 25 minutes.

Serve with either salad, jacket potatoes or your favourite vegetables."

(Shirley Barrass)

During the 1960's and '70s, many schoolgirls attended domestic science or home economics classes at school where they were taught, amongst other things, certain recipes. Paul's late wife, Shirley, was especially proud of her Tuna Plait recipe and it was produced on special occasions throughout her life.

Mum's Meat and Potato Pie

"This was served on a Saturday lunch in the wintertime with marrowfat mushy peas soaked overnight in water and bicarb.

Mum had a very large green pyrex mixing bowl that would go in the Rayburn.

She would start cooking this on a Thursday night as it was made from the meat from the bones of lambs or pork or sometimes beef bones.

She would put the bones in the mixing bowl with water, onions, carrots and an Oxo cube.

Into the Rayburn it went and cooked slowly overnight.

Next day it was taken out and put in the pantry (we didn't have a fridge) until it was cold. She would then pick all the meat off the bones and strain off the stock.

Peeled and chopped potatoes were added with onions until the bowl was full to the top. It was stirred well and more water added if needed.

It was then cooked again overnight in the Rayburn on a low heat and sat there until nearly lunchtime.

Peas were washed and brought to the boil to be cooked until soft and mushy.

For the suet crust, mum used 1lb self-raising flour, 8oz suet, a pinch of salt and enough water to make a dough-like consistency.

She would roll it out and place it on top of the (large green) mixing bowl then back into the Rayburn and cooked until slightly brown on top. Delicious!!

It was always a family favourite with my children and grandchildren but cooked in a slightly different way. Mine had meat cooked in the slow cooker and potatoes added. I still use Oxo cubes but I'm afraid I buy tinned mushy peas these days."

(Stephen Wagstaffe/Margaret Whitelaw)

Sausage Meat, Egg and Stuffing Pie made by my mum

"You make a pastry base, fill it with sausage meat, sliced boiled eggs and then a layer of sage and onion stuffing before finishing off the pastry case and cooking.

This was always a special treat on a Saturday which was baking day. We would make it as a family together (mum, dad, myself and my brother). We made things like sausage rolls, jam tarts and biscuits.

We did this on a Saturday before my grandfather came to visit for tea."

(Tracy Dineley)

Easy Sausage Stew

"This dish was made during war-time to feed a hungry family with four children.

I would be ten years old at the time. I am now 89 years young.

My dad used to chop up potatoes, onions and sausages and boil them in a pan until cooked. He would then add two Oxo cubes and thicken with cornflour.

This made a cheap, hot meal when food was rationed."

(Dee Winterbottom)

A Load of Bol

"This will make a large pan that will seem to last a week.

Minced beef
2 onions
1 green or red pepper
Mushrooms
2 cloves of garlic
2 tins chopped tomatoes
Olive oil
Tomato puree
Black pepper
Chilli seeds
Red wine
2 bay leaves
Pasta - spaghetti or penne
Grated cheese - Mozzarella or cheddar

The sauce:

Peel and dice the onions.

Chop the pepper.

Quarter the mushrooms.

Brown the mince in a frying pan with a small amount of olive oil.

Stir in black pepper to taste.

Add the onions until lightly fried.

Season with a small amount of salt.

Transfer to a large pan.

Add the peppers and cook until soft.

Add the mushrooms and cook until soft.

Pour in one can of chopped tomatoes and stir.

Add crushed garlic.

Pour in second can of chopped tomatoes and stir.

Add bay leaves.

Add a sprinkle of chilli seeds.

Pour in an egg cup of red wine and drink the rest.

Squeeze or spoon in some tomato puree. Do this gradually until the sauce thickens to a consistency you like.

Leave to simmer on lowest heat for 20 minutes.

The sauce can be left to stand all day if made for later, just reheat thoroughly.

The pasta:

Follow the instructions on the packet.

Rinse with boiling water and arrange on plate/bowl.

The sauce and pasta:

Pour the sauce over the pasta and add grated cheese.

Provenance

This recipe was developed, over time, by swapping the ingredients in a tin of pre-made Bolognaise with fresh ingredients. For over 30 years I have been making this dish convinced I was cooking a bolognaise as enjoyed by coastal countries around the Apennine Peninsula. Sometimes with or without the mushrooms or pepper, and sometimes swapping the beef for bacon. I would scoff it with spaghetti (and wine) thinking I was eating an Italian Spaghetti Bolognaise. Recently I worked with someone who is Italian and our conversation came around to food and I mentioned my "Italian" dish. Julius Caesar, on landing and tripping up on the south shores of Britannia, could not have given a more shocked Italian stare. Apparently, the traditional ingredients for a bolognaise sauce include carrot and celery. They (empathically and with gestures) do not include peppers or mushrooms, and tomatoes are not allowed anywhere near. Especially the pureed type. Not even passata."

(Mike Haynes, resident of land-locked Staffordshire)

Cheesy-Eggy Things

What can be quicker, tastier and easier than a dish made with eggs and cheese? It is a great way to use up stale bread. Day-old bread is often used, both for its thrift and because it will soak up more egg mixture without falling apart.

Cheesy Eggy food can be either an everyday food or made for a special occasion. I must admit that one of my favourite meals is simply poached eggs on toast.

Cheesy Eggy Thing on Toast

"Mix a soft-boiled egg and grated cheese in a mug while toasting one slice of bread.

Add mixed herbs then spread over the un-toasted side. Place under the grill with a sprinkling of pepper.

I remember my dad making this for a quick lunch on a cold day when I nipped home from school."

(James Green)

Cheese and Onion Casserole

"My father worked late and missed tea times, we had an Aga cooker and cheap cheese offcuts and rind ends were often made good use of. Mum made a dish with alternate layers of cheese and onion which she cooked in the regular oven and

25

left to stay hot in the slower oven. It was always ready to be served however late dad came home."

(Richard Pyle)

Cheese, Broccoli and Mushroom Pasta Bake

"This is the recipe that saved my life during my pioneering vegetarian days.

Midway through 1980 I was forced to change trains in Trowbridge, Wiltshire right alongside the station but never having stopped there before hadn't realised that the pigs were slaughtered on site.

I must have only sat there alone in the dark for about 20 minutes but it felt like an eternity as the pigs squealed into the night in the condemned cell.

As I boarded my next train, I realised that there would be no more Bowyers Pork Pies in my shopping bag and before long this extended to all meat items.

"And then there was trouble". What is an 18 year-old bloke supposed to eat now? Back then there were no pre-packaged Linda McCartney/Quorn sausages or burgers. It all had to be done from scratch.

When I went to a work's meal, there were no meatless dishes on the menu at all. Basil would sidle up alongside the table and as he wrung his hands he would say "We could rustle up an omelette for Sir". Being a veggie back then was just one up from witchcraft and I was indeed ducked in the River Avon on a couple of occasions.

My salvation was dear old Mary in the office who set me on my way with his simple, protein-rich dish that quite literally saved my veggie bacon on many occasions.

250g fusilli pasta
200g mature English Cheddar or more if you like it very cheesy
1 medium broccoli
1 punnet of mushrooms
1 tin chopped tomatoes

Simmer the pasta for around 10 minutes or so it is not over-soft.

At the same time steam the broccoli gently. Again, not too soft.

In the meantime, grate all the cheese.

Once the pasta is drained off mix all the ingredients in a large bowl or pan then transfer to an open-topped casserole dish.

Bake in the oven for about 40 minutes or a little longer if you like it crispier.

Ideally leave the last of the grated cheese to make a layer on top of the mixture before you pop it in the oven."

(Rick Reader)

Cheese and Onion Tart

"Soften onions in milk.

Add cheese and melt while still keeping some chunks of cheese solid.

Use a slotted spoon to strain the cheese and onion into a pastry case with a pastry lid on top.

Bake in the oven until golden. It is delicious hot or cold. Mum was famous for her cheese and onion tart which was baked on a plate – whatever size was handy. No one had posh baking tins. Yorkshire puddings could be made in a frying pan.

People were more inventive in those days. But for me the very special thing was to drink the "gravy" which was the cheesy, onion milk mixture.

I also used to drink cabbage water after cabbage was being cooked in a pan. I would season it with white pepper. No one had posh black pepper back then."

(Derrick Sharpe)

Eggy Bread or French Toast

I remember my mum making this as a quick and easy tea-time meal. She used to call it French Toast. Very posh especially when cut into dainty little fingers. Opinion was divided as to whether it was better with brown sauce or tomato ketchup. I was a brown sauce devotee whereas my brother enjoyed the red stuff.

Dip a slice of white bread into beaten egg and fry on both sides until golden. Easy peasy!

When I went off to university and lived in a shared house, I discovered that in different parts of the country there are different ways of cooking "eggy bread". Some people simply break an egg onto a slice of bread and cook it that way. Whereas others pick a hole in the middle of a slice of bread and eat it. They then crack an egg into the middle of the hole and fry it, keeping the yolk whole. This is sometimes called "egg in the basket" and if you decide to keep the bread from the middle of the slice and place it on top of the cooked yolk, behold! "Egg in the basket with a hat or lid".

I have heard of others putting finely chopped onion in with the beaten egg or making sweet eggy bread using sugar and cinnamon then serving it with fruit. Alternatively, a whole cheese sandwich can be coated with egg and fried, thus making a dish that is greater than the sum of its parts.

Cheesy Eggs

*"2 eggs
Cheese, grated
Mushrooms and tomatoes optional, sliced*

Grease an ovenproof dish.

Put eggs in dish and place under grill till white shows.

Put tomatoes, mushrooms and cheese on and put back under the grill till desired texture.

The above dish was what my mother did for me as I never ate potatoes until my later years."

(Mrs V Wilson)

Welsh Raerbit/Rarebit or Rabbit

There is some suggestion that Welsh rabbit derives from a South Wales Valleys staple, in which a generous lump of cheese (in lieu of rabbit) is placed into a mixture of beaten eggs and milk, seasoned with salt and pepper, and baked in the oven until the egg mixture has firmed and the cheese has melted. Onion may be added and the mixture would be eaten with bread and butter and occasionally with the vinegar from pickled beetroot.

Hannah Glasse, in her 1747 cookbook *The Art of Cookery*, gives recipes for "Scotch rabbit", "Welsh rabbit" and two versions of "English rabbit".

To make a Scotch rabbit, toast the bread very nicely on both sides, butter it, cut a slice of cheese about as big as the bread, toast it on both sides, and lay it on the bread.

To make a Welsh rabbit, toast the bread on both sides, then toast the cheese on one side, lay it on the toast, and with a hot iron brown the other side. You may rub it over with mustard.

To make an English rabbit, toast the bread brown on both sides, lay it in a plate before the fire, pour a glass of red wine over it, and let it soak the wine up. Then cut some cheese very thin and lay it very thick over the bread, put it in a tin oven before the fire, and it will be toasted and browned presently. Serve it away hot.

Or do it thus. Toast the bread and soak it in the wine, set it before the fire, rub butter over the bottom of a plate, lay the cheese on, pour in two or three spoonfuls of white wine, cover it with another plate, set it over a chafing-dish of hot coals for two or three minutes, then stir it till it is done and well mixed. You may stir in a little mustard; when it enough lays it on the bread, just brown it with a hot shovel.

Served with an egg on top, a Welsh rarebit is known as a *buck rabbit* or a *golden buck*.

Welsh rarebit blended with tomato (or tomato soup) is known as Blushing Bunny.

My version of Welsh Raerbit uses up mashed potatoes from Sunday lunch and therefore makes a delicious Sunday teatime meal. Mix leftover mashed potatoes with grated cheese. Add salt, pepper and Worcester sauce. Pile onto bread which has been toasted on the bottom side and grill until warmed through and the cheese has melted. Delicious and economical.

My mother in law used to use up leftover cheese sauce on toast under the same name.

Flavourings can include beer, mustard, cayenne pepper, paprika, garlic or Worcester sauce. I have even seen recipes which use ham or anchovies. This is a dish which had its humble origins as a peasant meal and is now enjoying almost celebrity status on menus as a trendy lunch or brunch dish. One step up from cheese on toast.

Soups and Stews

Warming, hearty soups and stews evoke memories of winter pleasures, family and comfort. The final meal is never the same twice as the ingredients change according to what is available. Again, regional and family variations abound. Irish stew, Scotch Broth, Lobby, Cullen Skink, Scouse among a multitude of others.

I have a memory of visiting my great grandma in Rochdale when she was very old. She had made a "bucket" of stew on the range and it was my first introduction to brown sauce (HP of course). Now, to me, a stew has to be accompanied by brown sauce to taste good.

A good stew often has a "mystery ingredient" whether it be a dash of Worcestershire sauce, Hellman's relish, Tabasco or Maggis sauce. This seems to bring the flavours to life and enhance the legend.

Grandma's Secret Recipe Soup

"This makes a large pot full.

You will need:
1 large onion cut up
4 carrots cut up
2 sticks celery cut up
4 large potatoes cubed
3 leeks cut up

Wash all the veg and put into a large pan with water to cover plus a bit more. Once boiled add a cupful of lentils and $\frac{1}{2}$ cupful barley which has previously been soaked to remove starch then rinsed.

Add salt and pepper and a splash of Maggis sauce.

Boil and simmer for at least half an hour or until the lentils and barley are soft.

You then need to add either hot dog sausages sliced, or German sausage or smoked sausage. Ham or quorn could also be used. The soup will be very thick.

The final touch is a good dollop of butter in the soup to add flavour.

This recipe has been in my family for over 50 years. I have made it for 33 years. My daughter has recently asked me for the recipe.

The secret is the Maggis sauce and the butter but the true secret is it got my girls eating vegetables from a very early age.

It's a great winter warmer served with crusty bread."

(Julie Sinclair Rule)

Goode Tomato Soup

"6oz carrots
8oz potatoes
1 leek
1 celery stalk
2 -3 bacon rashers with rind
2lb tomatoes with stalks
$\frac{1}{2}$ tsp pepper
2 tsp salt
Basil (to taste)
Water

Finely chop all the above ingredients (peeling the carrot and potatoes).

Add water, bring to boil then simmer until carrots and potatoes are soft.

Blend and add basil to taste.

Goode is my Grandfather's family name ... We are now 4th generation tomato growers. My "Dad Joe" passed away when I was 4 years old but I have fond memories of his greenhouse and wine cellar! I have been told stories about him getting prescriptions off the chemist and crushing them up and feeding them to the tomatoes. I love this recipe because it is so simple and can be made from all home grown produce."

(Linda Reed)

Pea and Ham Soup with Suet Dumplings

"Peas
Ham
Suet
Mint
Water
Salt
Flour
Baking Powder

My grandma used to make it when I was a child. She alone knew the recipe and I have warm memories of eating this."

(Daniel Lee)

Scottish Tattie Soup

"This is a really basic hearty soup my Nanna used to make. It was one of her family's regular meals and was a boon to her mother when feeding a large family. Given how basic are the ingredients in this rationing-friendly soup, it's flavoursome and satisfying. I've given a variant on the recipe too which my other grandmother (Gran) used to make for us to sit down with in the kitchen on a cold day.

Butter and oil for frying
1 chopped onion
A few carrots, sliced
A few potatoes cut into chunks

Stock cubes and water
A good handful of beef mince
Salt and pepper to taste
You can add seasonal veg as you like – neeps (swede) was favourite with my Nanna and sometimes leek or finely diced celery.

Fry the veg in butter/oil until they are starting to soften.

Add water or stock. Simmer for 40 minutes and season to taste. Only add the mince after the water is boiling or it colours the broth which should be light and clear in colour."

Gran's Vegetable Broth

"Similar to the above, only dice the vegetables smaller. There is also no mince in it and you need to add a handful of pearl barley. This produces a thicker soup and if you add mutton, it would be a classic Scotch broth."

(Amber Peacock)

Parsnip Soup with Honey

"I stumbled across this soup a few years ago and it has easily become one of my favourites. It's really simple, cheap and tastes great, as long as you like parsnips of course. The honey brings a little sweetness which is perfect on a cold winter's day.

With this recipe, it's not just one memory that stands out in particular but many small ones. Like for example the first time I made this for my girlfriend. It really impressed her and we are still together three years on. I think this soup may have had something to do with that.

The next time I made it for us was a little enthusiastic with the honey which turned it into a strange parsnip pudding. Not a pleasant experience.

My most recent experience of this dish comes from one of the occasions my mum came to visit me when I was living in London a year or so after I graduated from university. I was living for the first time in a reasonably presentable house and was looking to show her that I'd become a real adult with a nice house and that I could cook something more than beans on toast. So I thought I'd make this soup. My mum, after taking a mouthful, praised the soup and my cooking skills just as I had hoped she would. But after a minute or so, she looked at me and told me she was sorry, but she just really didn't like parsnips.

4-5 parsnips
1 medium potato
Vegetable stock cube
150ml single cream
Small tbsp honey
Salt and fresh black pepper

Peel and chop the parsnips and potato.

Put into a large pan with a stock cube and add boiling water until the veg is just covered. Bring to the boil and simmer until the veg is just cooked. Take off the heat for a few minutes and blend with a hand blender.

Add the cream and honey and stir through.

Leave on a low heat for another 5-10 minutes.

Season to taste and add an optional dash of cream to serve."

(Thomas Oldfield)

Mum's Lobby

"Left over beef
Stock
Potatoes
Carrots
Swede
Leek
Celery
Onion
Salt and pepper

Put the beef (diced), stock and onion in a saucepan.

Cook for about 1 hour then add chopped carrots, swede, leek and cook for another 30 minutes. Add potatoes, salt and pepper to taste and cook for a further 30 minutes.
Serve with crusty bread and red cabbage.

As a girl in the 1940's Monday was always washday. Mum would light the boiler first thing as washing took all day in those days.

On this day, Mum would make "Lobby", a dish made from leftover beef from the Sunday joint and very tasty it was, served with red cabbage and crusty bread.

It was cooked in a saucepan on a trivet over the fire. The fire grate was used to do all the cooking as it housed two ovens. We would come home to this lovely appetising meal after school. Happy memories."

(Valerie Haynes)

<u>Food inspired by other countries</u>

During the 20th century, food in Britain became more exciting, absorbing cuisines from other cultures like never before. Even though Indian curry was already popular in England in the 19th century and the first Indian restaurant opened in London in 1810. In fact, spices had been present in English cookery since the time of the Crusades in the late 11th century. Hannah Glasse's The Art Of Cookery Made Plain and Simple, first published in 1747, is one of the first cookbooks to give recipes for curries and pilaus.

I grew up in the 1960's and 1970's and my first taste of spice was from the Vesta range of Chow Mein and Beef Curry. Is was so popular that it is still available and bought today, not for its authentic flavour but, I suspect, for the memories it evokes.

'Meat and two veg' had been the staple diet for most families in the 1950's and 1960's. The average family rarely, if ever, ate out. The closest most people came to eating out was in the pub. There you could get potato crisps (three flavours only – potato, plain or salted – until Golden Wonder launched 'cheese and onion' in 1962), a pickled egg to go on top, and perhaps a pasty or some cockles, winkles and whelks from the seafood man on a Friday, Saturday or Sunday evening.

Things started to change when the UK's answer to the burger bars in America arrived in the 1950's to cater for that new group of consumers, the 'teenagers'. The first

Wimpy Bars opened in 1954 selling hamburgers and milkshakes and proved extremely popular.

The late 1950's and 1960's saw a rise in immigration from the former British colonies. And with them came at last...flavour!!

Although the first Chinese restaurant in London was opened in 1908, the real spread of Chinese restaurants began in the late 1950's and 1960's with the influx of migrants from Hong Kong. These proved very popular; indeed in 1958 Billy Butlin introduced chop suey and chips into his holiday camps!

The 1960's also saw a dramatic rise in the number and spread of Indian restaurants in Britain, especially in London and the South East. During rationing it had been very difficult if not near impossible, to obtain the spices required for Indian cooking but with the rise in immigration from the Indian subcontinent and the end of rationing, this was no longer a problem and the restaurants flourished.

Vesta Chow Mein

"*The most exotic meal we had was Vesta Chow Mein – completely different from meat and two veg or anything cooked by mum.*

It was a special treat.

Watching the flat noodles drop down into the fat fryer and suddenly crisp up, bubble and curl.

Snipping the plastic sachet of soya sauce and tasting it.

The dried sort of vegetables coming to life."

(Ang Stanyon)

Bigos

"I remember having this every week at the Polish club. There would be a big pot of it in the middle of the table and everyone would tuck in. Warm, happy memories.

I still cook this regularly today.

A round cabbage, shredded
2 carrots and 2 onions sliced
Tomato puree
A jar of sauerkraut, drained and rinsed

Put it all in a pan and boil for 2 hours."

(Lucy Elliot)

Bigos is considered a Polish national dish, traditionally, stewed in a cauldron over an open fire

Roasted Mushroom Risotto

"This has become somewhat of a tradition. When asked what a member of the family would like for their birthday tea (we always have a family birthday tea and a cake) everyone always seems to choose this one over anything else... so for the last five years we've had this for every single person's birthday tea. It is exceptionally tasty though!

You will need:
1 small onion finely chopped
2 sticks celery, trimmed and finely chopped
400g risotto rice
75ml vermouth or white wine
Sea salt
Freshly ground black pepper
350-400g mushrooms cleaned and chopped
2 cloves garlic finely chopped
A few sprigs fresh thyme, leaves picked and chopped
Juice of 1 lemon
1 tsp butter
1 small handful parmesan cheese, freshly grated plus extra for serving
Extra virgin olive oil
1.5 litres organic chicken or vegetable stock, hot
1 handful dried porcini mushrooms (optional)
Olive oil

Put chopped mushrooms, garlic and thyme into a baking tray, sprinkle liberally with olive oil and roast until cooked through.

Whilst the mushrooms cook, heat the stock in a saucepan and keep it on a low simmer. Place the porcini mushrooms in a bowl and pour in just enough hot stock to cover. Leave a couple of minutes until they've softened. Fish them out of the stock and chop them, reserving the soaking liquid.

In a large pan, heat a glug of olive oil and add the onion and celery. Slowly fry without colouring them for at least 10 minutes, then turn up the heat and add rice. Give it a stir. Stir in the wine or vermouth – it will smell fantastic! Keep stirring until the liquid has been absorbed into the rice. Now pour in the porcini soaking liquid through a sieve into a pan and add the chopped porcini, a good pinch of salt and your first ladle of hot stock. Turn the heat down to a simmer and keep adding ladlefuls of stock, stirring and massaging the starch out of the rice, allowing each ladleful to be absorbed before adding the next.

Carry on adding the stock until the rice is soft but with a slight bite. This will take about 30 mins. Meanwhile get a dry griddle pan hot and grill the wild mushrooms until soft. If your pan isn't big enough, do them in batches. Put them into a bowl and add the chopped herbs, a pinch of salt and the lemon juice. Using your hands, get stuck in and toss everything together. This is going to be incredible!

Take the risotto off the heat and check seasoning carefully. Stir in the butter and the parmesan. It needs to be creamy and oozy in texture, so add a bit more stock if you think it needs it. Put a lid on and leave the risotto to relax for about 3 minutes.

Take your risotto and add a little more seasoning or parmesan if you like. Serve a good dollop of risotto topped with some grilled dressed mushrooms, a sprinkling of freshly grated parmesan and a drizzle of extra virgin olive oil."

(Linden Weaver)

Creamy Garlic Mushrooms on Toast

"My fondest memories of making this is from the last few years of my nan's life while she was staying with us. She struggled to eat much due to her chemotherapy but it always brought a smile to her face when I made her this.

You will need:
$\frac{3}{4}$ medium tub of mushrooms, sliced

Fry in a pan with 2 tbsp garlic puree until soft.

When soft, pour in double cream to preference and season.

Serve on a thick slice of toast and top with parmesan cheese."

(Luke Yates)

Jamaican Rice and Peas

"Rice and Peas was a major staple in my family when I was young. A Sunday roast might have the usual English things in it (meat and two veg, Yorkshire puds, roast potatoes, gravy etc.) but for us, it was not a proper meal without rice.

Big family meals at Nana's house would have a big pot of rice, along with belly pork, Boiler Chicken, Curry Goat, and a pile of Hardo bread. Everyone helped with the cooking so I remember sitting on the sofa with my cousins preparing veg including a mountain of Brussel sprouts!

When I say rice and peas, I don't mean a pile of plain rice with some garden peas on the side. Beans are cooked in with the rice along with coconut, bacon and seasoning veg to make a great flavour.

Everyone has their preference about what goes in, and arguments can get heated! My Nana always made this with Basmati rice and red kidney beans (which turns it purple), but I prefer my dad's choice of American long grain rice and Gungo beans which has a better texture though I change to Rosa Coco beans if available.

You will need:
2 cups American long grain rice
1 can peas (Gungo, Red Kidney, Black eye, which ever you prefer
Creamed coconut – about 1/3 pack
1 small onion halved

Half a pepper roughly torn
Chunk of cooking bacon
2 chopped cloves garlic
A sprig or two rosemary or thyme
2 tsp salt

Empty the peas including liquid from the pan into a saucepan.

Add a full can of water.

Add everything else (except the rice) and bring to the boil.

Add the rice and keep boiling for two minutes.

Turn the fire to low, cover and cook until done – about 15 minutes."

(David Beckford)

Spaghetti Bolognaise

"I remember eating this when I was 7 years old in Italy, sucking up the long strands of sauce-soaked spaghetti and it splattering all over the place.

The Italians were a bit horrified, but indulgent as I was a foreigner and didn't know how to eat it politely. So they laughed in embarrassment which I took for encouragement and kept on doing it making a real mess."

(Ros Clark)

BBQ Spare Ribs

"We have my BBQ Spare Ribs every time we hold a barbeque or even on a cold, frosty day. My mum used to be in the kitchen making them and once they had cooled down after cooking, my sister and I would sneak in and eat spoonfuls of the sauce, Happy memories.

This is a recipe which has passed down from my nana to my mum and now to my sister and me. My son also loves them.

You will need:
2 tbsp vegetable oil
1 crushed garlic clove
Large onion finely chopped
5 fl oz tomato juice
3 tbsp lemon juice
$\frac{1}{2}$ tsp salt
$\frac{1}{4}$ tsp black pepper
$\frac{1}{2}$ tsp dried sage
4 tbsp light brown sugar
4 fl oz beef stock
4 tbsp Worcestershire sauce
2 tsp dried mustard
3lbs spare ribs of pork cut into serving pieces"

(Johanna Alice Pender Orridge)

Some place the origin of barbecue sauce at the formation of the first American colonies in the 17th century. References to the substance start occurring in both English and French literature over the next two hundred years. South Carolina mustard sauce, a type of barbecue sauce, can be traced to settlers in the 18th century.

Early cookbooks did not tend to include recipes for barbecue sauce. The first commercially produced barbecue sauce was made by the Georgia Barbecue Sauce Company in Atlanta, Georgia. Its sauce was advertised for sale in the Atlanta Constitution, January 31, 1909. Heinz released its barbecue sauce in 1940. Kraft Foods also started making cooking oils with bags of spice attached, supplying another market entrance of barbecue sauce.

Spanish Omelette

"As a child and an adult, I remember going to Spain on holiday with my mum who was Spanish. My aunties, and later on my cousins would often make this omelette and even take it out as a sandwich filler on days out to Madrid or Toledo. This is very filling, easy to make and always brings back fond memories.

A true Spanish omelette has only 3 ingredients.

You will need:
1-2 medium potatoes – sliced
2 sliced onions
3 eggs
Salt and pepper

Heat olive oil in a medium frying pan. When really hot, fry the sliced potatoes and onions – enough to fill the pan. Cover and cook until very soft. You can even use cold, leftover potatoes.

Meanwhile, beat the eggs in a bowl and season. Add the potatoes and onions to the eggs and mix well.

Heat more oil in the pan and when hot add the egg mixture to the pan. While cooking, shake and tap the sides. This will stop it sticking.

When the bottom of the omelette is cooked, upturn a large plate over the pan and carefully turn the omelette over and place it back in the pan. Do this at least twice more and that way it will cook properly.

DO NOT cheat and put it under the grill as it won't cook properly and doesn't taste the same. It can be eaten on its own, with a salad, as a sandwich filler in a baguette or as tapas."

(Lucy Elliott)

Paella

"My wife, Lucy, and I went to Spain to see her Spanish family in 2000. One of her aunts showed me how to cook an authentic paella. I watched carefully and tried cooking one a few weeks after returning home to Derby. Upon eating my first ever paella, Lucy said to me "This is better than mine. You can cook it from now on."

Ideally it should be cooked on an outside fire as a paella pan is too big to fit on a normal hob. Newspaper of cardboard should be placed on the table to protect it from the soot on the bottom of the pan.

A good glug of olive oil
A full bulb of garlic peeled and chopped
Chicken or fish diced
2 tsp pimento or paprika (smoked or not)
Colerante or saffron – enough to colour the food
Salt
Prawns
Peas or beans
2 teacups paella rice
Enough boiling water to cover the food plus extra to top up during cooking
One lemon

Fry the garlic in olive oil.

Fry the meat or fish.

Then add all the other ingredients except the lemon.

Bring to the boil and simmer until cooked.

You may need to add more water.

Once cooked put wedges of lemon around the outside.

You can have just meat with this dish, or fish or vegetables. Whatever you fancy or have to hand."

(Jim Elliott)

Offally Good Meals

I have found accounts of the North West's 146 tripe shops where you could eat in or take away offal-based products. (Courtesy of unitedcattleproducts.co.uk)

"U.C.P. The initials stood for United Cattle Products - advertised as "the offal emporium of the north-west." The U.C.P. sold much more than just the load of tripe my mother bought. There was cow heels and black pudding, brawn, heart, ox tongue, and sweetbreads, liver, kidneys, rissoles, faggots, sausage and many more bovine delights. I remember this shop and cafe very well. Saturday mornings I would be dragged around Hyde while mum did some 'week end' shopping. Everything else she would buy during the week was from our local Spar shop at the bottom of Knott Lane when she could 'run up a slate'. The Spar's long gone and is now known as Grocer Jacks, and very well it seems to be doing as well... but let's get back to Saturday mornings of old. After some shopping, mum would head to the U.C.P. to meet up with my very scary Granny Wig and my Aunty Annie. At the table would be another two ladies whose names I don't recall. It was a sorry looking bunch, never a smile between them, but we had to turn up on Saturday for any gossip. I hated it... Apart from the food, their chips and gravy were to die for. Sometimes I got pie & chips but my favourite was their steamed puddings. We always sat downstairs and I never did see the inside of the much posher upstairs. I did see the ladies who served upstairs though, and very smart they looked to in their black uniforms, white bonnets, and

white apron. Mum always bought her tripe before she left. The stall was enough to give you nightmares and the names it went by were not much better - elder, honeycomb, thick seam, bag, slut, brown... the list goes on. As far as I know I've never knowingly ate it, but mum was a pest at putting different stuff on our plates. Brawn was something else she tried feeding us on, and for years those cold beef butties I liked so much turned out to be ox heart... I don't eat offal at all now... if I can help it!"

Savoury Ducks

"Being brought up on a farm when I was about 4 or 5 years old, my grandad (Fred Gibson) used to be a slaughterman. I remember when my auntie Winifred, my mum and dad used to make Savoury Ducks out of the offal.

They were delicious and tasted a bit like Haslet.

Cut the lights and heart into small pieces. Wash well in salt water and put in a pan with water to cook for about 2 hours.

Add 2lbs onions and boil again for 30 minutes.

Cut up half a loaf of bread into squares, put them in a pan to soak.

Put the mixture through the mincer then into a large dish.

Add salt, pepper and sage to season.

Mix 2 or 3 tablespoons of plain flour with water to a smooth paste and add a little gravy browning.

Pour the flour and gravy browning mixture into the dish with the savoury ducks and stir until thickens.

Put the mixture into the skins of the offal.

Put into greased tins and bake in a moderate oven until cooked."

(Stephen Wagstaffe/Margaret Whitelaw)

Pork Chitterlings

"Pork Chitterlings
Vinegar
Pepper
Salad

My mother used to buy chitterlings from the pork butcher. They were a special treat and were delicious. Washed intestines turned inside-out, cleaned, plaited and boiled. Usually sold cooked and chilled, sometimes in their own jelly, to be eaten cold with vinegar and mustard, or fried with bacon."

(Doreen Whelbourne)

Liver and Onions

900g sliced beef liver
350ml milk, or as needed
55g butter, divided
2 large Spanish onions, sliced into rings
250g plain flour, or as needed
Salt and pepper to taste

Gently rinse liver slices under cold water, and place in a medium bowl. Pour in enough milk to cover. Let stand while preparing onions. (I like to soak up to an hour or two - whatever you have time for.) This step is SO important in taking the bitter taste of the liver out.

Melt 2 tablespoons of butter in a large pan over medium heat. Separate onion rings and cook them in butter until soft. Remove onions and melt remaining butter in the pan. Season the flour with salt and pepper and put it in a shallow dish or on a plate. Drain milk from liver and coat slices in the flour mixture.

When the butter has melted, turn the heat up to medium-high and place the coated liver slices in the pan. Cook until nice and brown on the bottom. Turn and cook on the other side until browned. Add onions and reduce heat to medium. Cook a bit longer to taste. Our family prefers the liver to just barely retain a pinkness on the inside when you cut to check. Enjoy!

Steak and Kidney Pudding

1oz/25g beef drippings (or lard or vegetable oil)
1 1/2lbs/675g beef topside (cut into 2.5cm/1-inch cubes)
12oz/350g beef kidney (cut into 2.5cm/1-inch cubes)
1 onion (peeled and roughly chopped)
2 carrots (washed, peeled and thickly sliced)
1oz/25g all-purpose flour
10 fl oz/300ml beef stock
5 fl oz/150ml red wine
1 bay leaf
1 small handful flat leaf parsley (finely chopped)
1 tbsp tomato puree
Salt and pepper to taste

For the pastry:

10oz/280g self-raising flour
1/2 tsp baking powder
Pinch of salt
5oz/140g beef suet (finely chopped)
2 to 3 tbsp cold water
3 tbsp butter for greasing
2 sheets of greaseproof paper

Preheat the oven to 350 F/180 C. Heat a large casserole dish on the stove, add the drippings/lard or oil and heat until slightly smoking. Add the beef cubes and the kidney, stir well until all the meat is browned. Add the onion, carrots, and stir again.

Sprinkle the flour over the meat and vegetables and stir thoroughly.

Add the stock, red wine, bay leaf, parsley, and tomato puree. Bring to a gentle boil, then reduce the heat and cover with a lid. Place in the hot oven and cook for 1 hour.

Remove the casserole from the oven, season with salt and pepper to taste, and leave it to cool.

Make the pastry. Place the flour, baking powder, and salt into a baking bowl. Add the suet and rub into the flour. Add enough cold water to form a stiff, slightly sticky dough. Leave it to rest for 30 minutes.

Grease a 2-pint pudding basin with the butter. Divide the pastry into 2/3 and 1/3 parts and roll the larger piece of dough into a circle large enough to line the basin with an extra 1/2" border. Dust your hands with a little flour then carefully line the basin with the dough.

Add the meat mixture and roll the remaining dough into a circle large enough to make a lid. Wet the overhanging lip of the basin with cold water, lay the lid on top and press firmly around the edge to seal.

Cover the basin with two circles of greaseproof paper secured with kitchen string.

Steam over rapidly boiling water for 2 hours. Check frequently to make sure water has not boiled dry. Top up with boiling water as needed.

Remove the pudding from the steamer, remove the greaseproof paper, and serve.

The increasing employment of women during the 20th century meant that long-winded recipes requiring preparation and slow cooking were simply no longer practical. The flavours of this classic dish remained, however, in the form of the easier to make steak and kidney pie – plus, of course, in Fray Bentos's tinned version, a 1970s culinary institution that is still available today. Ready-made pudding in a tin. Just imagine how excited the Victorians would have been about that.

Faggots

1lb 2oz pig's liver, lungs and heart, diced
1lb 2oz pork belly
2 onions, diced
Few fresh sage leaves, chopped
Few fresh thyme sprigs, leaves picked
2 garlic cloves, minced
6 fresh bay leaves
$10\frac{1}{2}$oz caul fat
$1\frac{3}{4}$pints dark chicken stock

Bring a large pan of water to the boil and add the diced meat. Return to the boil, then drain the meat and set aside to cool.

Preheat the oven to 150C/300F/Gas 2.

Mince the meat, add it to a bowl and stir in the onion, herbs and garlic until well combined.

Shape the mixture into six balls, lay a small bay leaf on top and wrap in the caul fat.

Sit the faggots in a roasting tray and pour in the stock. Cook the faggots in the oven for one hour.

Run, Rabbit, Run

Wild Rabbit and other game have always been used as ingredients in delicious stews, pies and casseroles. Especially if you lived in the countryside, these meats were more freely available than if you lived in the town or city.

I remember growing up in a country pub and one of the customers used to regularly bring a freshly killed rabbit for my brother to clean and skin. We never had to buy a vegetable as long as we lived there as some customers would pay off their bar bills with bags of fresh vegetables (and the odd rabbit).

In Hallaton, Leicestershire this is an ancient custom with two distinct parts. The first is a charity dole and the second is a mass "ballgame" played with small wooden casks called bottles. The fun starts with a procession from the Fox Inn through the village, led by the Warrener with his hare-topped staff and his attendants with baskets of bread and the eponymous Hare Pie (I believe it is minced beef these days). The Bottles, be-ribboned, filled with ale and each weighing 5 kg, are carried by three strong players. Once at the church gate, the pie is blessed and distributed to the crowd; the Procession then returns to the Buttercross in the centre of the village where the loaves are given out and then goes back to the Fox. A break follows then it all starts up again with another Procession, this time to Hare Pie Bank where the game takes place. Play is between the villagers of Hallaton and their neighbours from Medbourne and the goals are a mile apart; the bottles are thrown in the air and a fierce contest begins. Injuries are fairly common as the scrum heaves across the fields, over any obstacles including fences and streams in its path. Play can continue after dark and the game is decided by the best of three bottles. There are few rules!

Tim's Mum's "Chicken Stew"

*"Take one rabbit (which is always called chicken) shot by Dad
Remove shotgun pellets
Carrots and onion
Dumplings (so called because the suet was overcooked until it was as hard as rubber)*

Make a stew.

I remember this stew as being hot and filling. However, Mum is an awful cooker of vegetables. They were boiled to death and bicarb added to give the veg a zing!

The stew was a bit of a lucky dip as there was usually a mouthful of shot per meal.

It is always useful to have a golden retriever or Labrador to hand as they eat anything left over."

(Tim Adcock)

Milky Rabbit Casserole

"Rabbit Joints
Onion
1 rasher bacon
2 carrots
1 pint milk
Seasoning
$\frac{1}{4}$ tsp nutmeg
$\frac{1}{2}$ oz cornflour
2 tbsp milk

Rabbit, pigeon, pheasant were part of our meal, often with pellets left in. We also had our own pigs. All parts of the pig were used. Mother made brawn with the trotters. Lots of stews. The bladder was blown up for my brother to use as a football. We also had milk straight from the cow and Mother would make a pudding with "breastings" (the first milk from a cow after calving). All vegetables were grown in our own garden. Chickens, eggs would often hatch in front of the store. We had pet cats, dogs, rabbits and ferrets."

(Elaine Wall)

Raised Game Pie

"Some few years ago, after an absence following work, we, that is my wife and I, decided to move back to the countryside, and to the area we both love, on the edge of the new forest, south of Salisbury – you know the city, the Russians love it, especially the 330 steps in the spire.

Well, having lived in the very beautiful village before, it was time to meet and greet old friends, and the best place to do that is in the local public house over a pint of beer or three.

I got talking to a very dear friend in particular, and the subject of country sports came up, and the next thing I knew I was a guest on the river Test trying to look as if I know what I was doing with a Fly-fishing rod in my hand.

Well, a few months went past, and whilst my friend was away doing other things during the winter months, I found a local trout fishery where I could go and practice before the start of the following season.

So, there I was ready at the start of the following season, when my very good friend said "have you got a license", to which I immediately, and rather proudly, declared I did.

"Which one" he asks "shotgun or firearms?"

Apparently, it was time for me to take up arms against the local wildlife, being that I was living in the country.

As it happens, although I was taken somewhat by surprise by this, being a reenactor for many years and in the artillery, I answered (with a bit of smugness) "Yes – both".

This was the point where I was immediately purchasing weapons: "I've got two rifles for you. You can have 'em cheap"

"Oh, and please tell me you have a shotgun – I haven't got one of them for you, but you're going to need one."

I did.

Fortunately.

How embarrassing would it be for someone living in the countryside NOT to have a shotgun. Scandalous.

Oh, but we weren't finished yet.

"You've got a dog, of course."

"Yes, of course."

"What breed" he enquires.

Well what I didn't know was that there are only two breeds – Spaniel, and Labrador.

Rough Collie show dog doesn't count, with the exception that it produces great amusement. Another story, another time.

So now I am also the very proud owner of the sweetest little Labrador, the happiest dog in the whole world, and at still only 19 months old, the most remarkable retriever.

So, where on earth am I going with this (longer than expected) story?

Hunting and shooting brings many rewards, and one of those rewards is a full larder, and what do you do with a larder full of game meat? Why you make the most amazing Raised Game Pie ever imagined.

I hope you enjoy the slightly exaggerated story as much as you enjoy the pie.

To make the pie:

Equipment and preparation: you will need a 20cm/8in spring-form cake tin, about 7cm/2$\frac{3}{4}$in deep.

2 banana shallots, finely chopped
2 garlic cloves, crushed
700g/1lb 9oz mixed, boned, diced game meat, such as venison, rabbit, duck, pheasant, pigeon and boar (my personal favourite equal venison, duck and pheasant)
200g/7oz minced pork belly
200g/7oz back bacon, rind removed, diced
2 tbsp Madeira wine
$\frac{1}{2}$ tsp ground mace
$\frac{1}{2}$ tsp ground allspice
2 tbsp chopped parsley
2 tbsp chopped thyme
Salt and white pepper

For the hot water crust pastry:

450g/1lb plain flour
100g/3½oz strong white bread flour
75g/2½oz cold, unsalted butter, cut into roughly 1cm/½in dice
½ tsp salt
100g/3½oz lard, plus extra for greasing
1 free-range egg yolk, beaten, to glaze

Method:

1. Preheat the oven to 200C/180C Fan/Gas 6. Grease a 20cm/8in spring-form cake tin, about 7cm/2¾in deep, with lard.
2. First make the filling. In a large bowl, mix the shallots and garlic. Add the game, pork belly mince, diced bacon, Madeira, spices and herbs. Season with salt and a little white pepper.
3. Using your hands, mix all the ingredients thoroughly together. Put in the fridge while you prepare the pastry.
4. For the hot water crust pastry, combine the flours in a bowl, add the butter and rub in lightly with your fingertips.
5. Heat 200ml/7 fl oz of water, the salt and lard in a saucepan until just boiling. Pour the mixture onto the flour and mix together with a spoon. Once cool enough to handle, tip onto a floured surface and knead into a smooth dough.

6. Work as quickly as you can now (as the pastry will become more crumbly as it cools). Cut off two-thirds of the pastry, roll it out and use to line the prepared tin, leaving any excess hanging over the side. Check there are no cracks or holes in the pastry. Roll out the remaining pastry for the lid and leave to one side.
7. Spoon the filling into the pastry-lined tin. Press it down and level the surface.
8. Brush the pastry edge with beaten egg yolk and place the pastry lid on top. Crimp the edges to seal and trim off the excess pastry neatly. Brush the top with more egg yolk. Make a hole in the middle of the lid for steam.
9. Stand the tin on a baking tray and bake the pie for 30 minutes. Turn the oven down to 160C/140C Fan/Gas 3 and bake for a further $1\frac{3}{4}$ hours.
10. Leave the pie to cool completely in the tin before removing. Slice on a plate to catch any juices. Serve at room temperature."

(Jim Eames)

Irish Chicken

"1 large Irish Chicken, jointed
6 peeled potatoes, chopped
6 peeled carrots sliced
2 onions chopped
2 beef Oxo cubes
Salt and pepper
Water to cover

Batter mix using 4 eggs. Leave in pantry covered with cloth.
Beef dripping

Place everything in a lidded cast iron pot and slow cook on ashes of the range fire while parents are working and the kids are at school. First person home moves the pot to range oven and gets the fire going again.

While the fire is going well, move pot out of oven and place on oven ring.

Put a wooden spoon full of dripping into four 12" pudding tins and place in the oven. Once dripping is spitting, pour the batter into tins and place in the oven. Wait 20 minutes without opening the oven door. Open the door and let the steam escape. Close the door and cook for a further 10 minutes. The Yorkshire puddings will be golden and crisp on the outside but still soft and fluffy on the inside.

To serve:

Place one fluffy Yorkshire pudding on a plate and spoon the Irish chicken stew into the middle of the pudding.

My parents and grandparents used to make this. They all had cast iron ranges. I was 12 years old when we got our house modernised. I remember the builder removing the range with a sledge hammer. It never tasted the same cooked in a normal oven. And, yes, Irish chicken was a rabbit!"

(Simon Allen)

Round the Campfire

When it comes to food from around the campfire, anyone who was a member of scouts, guides, boys or girls' brigades will have memories of sharing meals cooked in the open air. Food is somehow extra tasty when cooked on an open wood fire or a barbeque after spending time outdoors, having adventures and exploring the world.

Banana Chocolate

Make a slit through the skin of the bananas along one side – making sure you don't cut all the way through to the other side.

Poke in chocolate buttons along the cut.

Put each banana onto a sheet of foil and crimp the edges together to seal into a parcel.

Cook in the BBQ embers for 15 minutes or until you cannot bear to wait any longer.

Remove carefully with a stick, unwrap and enjoy.

Cowboy Stew

6-8 good quality sausages
1 onion, chopped
4 cloves garlic, finely chopped

1 chilli, finely chopped
1 can mixed beans in water, drained
1 can tomatoes
1 can baked beans
Salt and pepper

Fry the sausages until well coloured.

Add the onions and sweat down until softened.

Tip in the chilli & garlic and fry for a couple more minutes.

Finally tip in the three cans, bring to a boil then cover and let simmer for 10-15 minutes or until the sauce has thickened and the sausages have cooked through. To stretch it to feed more, serve with rice, pasta or crusty bread.

Corned Beef Hash – Scout Campfire Version

"This is cooked on a wood fire in a billy can.

You will need:
Chopped onions
Chopped potatoes
Corned beef
Baked beans around the outside of the pan like a moat.

Everyone digs into the same pan with a spoon. Whoever eats quickest gets the most."

(Trevor Brearley)

Divine Hash

"1 tin corned beef
1 medium onion
3 medium potatoes
1 tin baked beans
Condiment sachets (the sort that could conceivably be purloined from Wetherspoons!)
A single pan

Why could such a simple and basic dish be described as Divine?

The taste is divine after a hard day climbing or hiking in the hills.

The sheer simplicity is simply divine.

There is an element of divine intervention.

This is truly a one pan meal, the only other utensils are a tin opener, a knife to chop up the veggies and a couple of spoons for you and a mate to eat with.

I say a one pan meal; in hiking and mountain climbing circles, we used to carry a small/medium billy pan with us on our exploits. Importantly, a billy pan came complete with a lid, and was perfect for carrying a small Primus Stove inside to save space in our rucksacks. The main body of the pan was usually used for boiling water, and the lid was a perfectly good frying pan that could also double up as a plate – that could even be put back on the stove to warm a meal back up again if it was really cold outside!

Method:

Go and find a spring, dip the pan in and half fill it with water. Alternatively, fill the pan completely with fresh snow, press it down and add some more snow.

Light the stove, put the pan on to melt the snow (if appropriate) and bring the water to the boil.

Hack up the potatoes into half inch cubes, feel free to leave the skin on for added flavour, and a bit of extra fibre for a bit towards your five-a-day.

Chuck the potatoes into the water and boil for ten to twelve minutes. If you like salted potatoes, rip open a couple of sachets – but this limits any future use of the water.

Peel the onion, unlike the potatoes, the skins don't really add to the flavour! Finely dice 'em and then chuck 'em into the billy pan lid.

Open the corned beef tin at both ends. Push the contents out onto the larger of the two lids. Scrape off the fat from the top of the corned beef and dob it into the billy lid with the onions. To be honest a bit more fat/oil would help here, but space and weight are important considerations for backpackers. Try and avoid scoffing the corned beef as it sits there looking at you – ok, may be have a small slice each.

Once the potato cubes have almost softened, spoon them out of the billy (against the side of the pan to drain 'em) into the pan lid with the onions and fat. Put the lid on the stove, and stir the chopped veggies until the onions have softened and the potatoes browned.

Lob the corned beef into the lid, breaking it up into lumps similar to the potatoes add some HP sauce and/or ketchup from your stash of sachets as required. Keep 'blending and folding' the amazing smelling mixture to avoid burning it to the lid.

Open the tin of baked beans. Applying the same rules to the corned beef, try to avoid scoffing 'em.

Now the delicate bit, gently pile the contents of the billy lid into a pyramid, complete with a moat. Pour whatever beans you have left into the moat, try to lower the heat of the Primus Stove (a bit of a challenge, as it requires a degree of dexterity to lower the pressure whist avoiding a minor explosion – something to really be averted if cooking in a tent, and a particular hazard for those sporting a beard!).

Try to 'stir' just the beans for a minute or so. Now empty the potato water into your tea mugs. Invert the billy pan, carefully placing it on top of its own lid. Turn off the heat, and try to wait for a few more minutes while the beans finish warming up.

Strategically place the steaming banquet on the floor 'between you and your mate - slightly nearer yourself! Sprinkle salt and pepper as required. Toss your mate a spoon in a way that can't easily be caught, allowing you to quickly tuck-in and maximise your share!!

Remember the potato water that you tipped in your mugs? Well tip it back into the billy pan, bring to the boil and add a tea bag. It might have a slightly different taste to what you may be used to (especially if you salted the water in paragraph three of the Method) but it means you're both conserving water and an extra bit of starch, which may help in any arduous climb first thing in the morning.

Taking the evening air before bedding down for the night

Feeling replete and a little drowsy, it was time to observe the setting sun and bask in the success of the valley views which evidenced the extent of the day's climbing.

Rather surprisingly, there was a tiny tent adjacent to our own abode, which we assumed had been amazingly pitched in silence while we were cooking. And, sat amongst the rocks was what looked like a terrifically old, bearded man with a ten year-old child as his companion. Naturally we assumed he'd struggled up the peak as a bonding exercise with his favourite grandson, possibly, his last big opportunity before infirmity eventually consigned him to gentle meadow walks.

Pausing for an opportunity, he casually and quietly asked us if we'd had a good day etc. and, naturally, we entered into a brief conversation about the trek thus far. As we discussed the weather there was significant change in the climate atop the mountain. Mist started to swirl about us and the temperature noticeably fell, the conversation concluded with a gentle enquiry about our route in the morning. Pulling a map from my breast pocket we studied our plans. The bearded face perceivably rocked from side to side, "It may not look it, but that descent really is steep, why not aim for this path just to the West, it's a bit easier and joins your route anyway." Clearly my initial, and maybe arrogant thoughts were somewhat rash. Here seemed to be a knowledgeable mountain man, passing on his experience to his family. I suspect he would be trekking these hills for longer than I'd first considered. Good wishes were exchanged and all parties prepared to retire for the night.

In the mountains, the morning light always seems to wake one early, even in thick fog. We made a cuppa, hydrated a portion of dried milk and muesli mixture, and a few minutes later we were outside packing our rucksacks. The old man, the ten year-old and their tiny tent had disappeared - as silently as they had materialised the previous evening. And I thought we'd got up early.

Pulling the map once more from one pocket, and my compass from another, a bearing was quickly set along the new route adopted under the old man's caution. Like mountain gazelles (a unique breed, only found our mountain!) we set off. Even down the more gentle path, the gradient required a degree of consideration in the mist.

After a careful descent of several hundred feet, we exited the cloud base that enveloped the mountain the previous evening. Glancing to over a shoulder, the route that we had been advised to avoid became evident: a sheer drop falling to the valley floor below us. The consequences of a chance meeting with the old mountain man who mysteriously emerged and then departed after imparting elemental counsel bought a lump to the throat, silencing further conversation for several hours. Divine intervention?"

(Trevor Brearley)

Proper Puddings

Memories of puddings tend to be warm and pleasant. Think of the types of puddings commonly available in the middle of the 20th century: milk puddings, suet puddings, set puddings and pastry-based pies and tarts. School meals were made compulsory in 1944 and always had some sort of sweet to follow. The object was to fill you up or, in the case of stodgy puddings, make it "stick to your ribs". The agenda was to build up the nation's workforce by enforcing minimum nutritional standards.

Many of the ingredients to make puddings had been rationed during the war so when the ingredients were again freely available, puddings were back on the menu.

Some children detested the rice pudding, tapioca or mysterious custard served in metal jugs at school and yet have glowing memories of sweet, sticky sensual puddings made by loving parents or grandparents.

Suet Pudding in a Basin

"This was my favourite pudding from my grandma. Put suet crust into a basin to line it and then fill with fresh fruit from the garden. Blackcurrants, raspberries, strawberries, apples and so on.

This was completed with a pastry top and covered with a cloth.

Boil for about 3 hours. Wonderful."

(Nancy Plummer)

Spotted Dick

"I remember my grandma making it. Boiling it in a muslin sheet tied with string at each end. I recall my dad used to love it especially cutting it open and unwrapping the pudding to reveal a brown centre with a white coating. We always had it with custard. I didn't like it as much as my dad."

(John Brettell)

Semolina Pudding with Home-Made Damson Jam

I remember eating this after smearing it around the plate mixing up the colours.

The damsons were always picked from the old tree in the garden. All the family had to join in with the harvesting. Mum made the jam with help from my sister and me.

Rice Pudding

"I remember my grandma making this every Saturday when we went to see her. Always made in an enamel dish with full fat milk and butter. My twin sister and I would always fight for the crust left after the pudding had gone. To scrape it

off was the best thing ever. It brings back such wonderful, comfortable memories of my grandma and her cooking."

(Sue Brettell)

Mum's Apple Crumble

"Apples
Flour
Butter or margarine

Rub into flour.

Peel and cut up apple.

You can vary with apples and blackberries, sultanas or whatever is to hand.

Place apples into the dish with white sugar.

Sprinkle on the crumble and cook at regulo 5 for 20 minutes.

Serve with custard.

I learned from my mum.

It was simple. We had a Keswick apple tree in the garden which blew down in a high wind in 2018. It was 120 years old. Keswick apples are not good keepers, so crumbles abounded in the apple season."

(Audrey Barrass)

I set a crumble on fire when I was a student. I had forgotten to put cinnamon in the mixture so sprinkled it on top of the crumble after it had cooked. I slipped it under a hot grill hoping it would brown a little more. Next thing I knew, flames were leaping from the grill.

Crumbles became popular in Ireland during World War II, when the topping was an economical alternative to pies due to shortages of pastry ingredients as the result of rationing. To further reduce the use of flour, fat and sugar, breadcrumbs or oatmeal could be added to the crumble mix. The dish was also popular due to its simplicity.

Trifle without Custard

"Trifle sponges liberally soaked on port
Fruit cocktail
Jelly
Angel delight
Cream
Mandarin oranges to decorate in a swirly pattern

I still make this and take it to Christmas family gatherings.

I never use custard as I detest anything with heated milk in the recipe so any trifle I make has to have Angel delight instead of custard."

(Vic James)

Apple Pie

"One and a half pounds Bramley apples
Gas 7 475 degrees
8oz self-raising flour
4oz lard – I use Trex
Pinch salt
Cold water

Mix the flour and lard together to an even crumbly texture.

Add the salt.

Mix to a soft dough with cold water.

I was taught this recipe as a girl at school in domestic science.

I looked forward to and enjoyed these lessons very much and I remember Miss Sheldon was our teacher.

Here's the apple pie recipe.

Mum forgot these bits of instructions that need adding in.

Pour 2 tablespoons of cold water over the peeled and sliced Bramley apples and add one heaped dessert spoon of white granulated sugar and slowly cook on a low gas flame in an open pan until soft but not mushy. Allow to cool completely.

Roll out the pastry to 1/8 inch thickness and fit to the size of an enamelled tin plate (approx. 8 inches in diameter). Do this twice for the base and lid of the pie.

Lightly grease the plate with lard and place the pastry slightly overhanging the edge. Trim the excess pastry off with a knife.

Moisten the edge with a small amount of water. This will help bind the lid and base together.

Evenly spread the apple filling over the base.

Place the pastry lid over the filling, trim the excess pastry off the edges and then crimp the pastry edge together using finger and thumb.

Slice three parallel 1 inch openings in the centre of the lid to allow vapour to escape.

Cook for 15 minutes.

Stand for 5 minutes.

Sprinkle with a teaspoon of white granulated sugar.

300 Years and 7,000 miles, There and Back Again

A trip to Virginia is something I recommend everyone should do as it is one of the finest parts of the world for natural beauty and hospitality. Small town America is a warm and friendly place and the lands around Washington DC and running down the Shenandoah are filled with abundant farms and comfort.

Local cuisine is always a temptation and it was with a keen appetite I anticipated my first taste of American homemade apple pie.

Of course, homemade is a bit of a stretch as the pie would be enjoyed in a restaurant, but it would be fresh and kitchen cooked rather than mass produced in some factory.

Cracker Barrel is a chain of Virginian restaurants that offer a country kitchen style of cuisine, and all the furniture is stoutly made of pinewood with checked cotton tablecloths. All very homely and promising. I was delighted to see "Homemade Apple Pie" on the menu and placed my order. I was not disappointed in the least. Home-made was a perfect description because my Mother had been baking this exact pie for over 70 years, every Sunday, following a roast beef dinner in Congleton, Cheshire. The apple pie was encased in sweet short crust pastry identical to Mum's and packed to the same depth with a juicy apple filling. No unnecessary cinnamon or raisins thrown in, just a light dusting of granulated sugar. It was completely identical in taste, texture and appearance.

At some point back in the 17th Century, families leaving England to settle in Virginia took with them all they knew to start a new life. Apple pie must have been a speciality of at least one good mother because it certainly crossed the Atlantic.

Enjoy the recipe and just think that you are tasting something that has been enjoyed for centuries

Good 'ole Cheshire Apple Pie, from the US of A."

(Valerie Haynes)

Bread and Butter Pudding

This is one of my favourite puddings. Another good use of leftover bread. Plain and simple with no additional flavourings. I have tried adding brandy, vanilla and using marmalade but I prefer the simple, unadulterated flavours. For me, the secret is to leave the bread and butter to soak up the egg mixture for a couple of hours before baking. That way, the bread becomes light and delicious while the top remains crispy.

Take 4 or 5 slices of thick day-old bread and butter thickly.

Cut in half or quarters and lay in an ovenproof dish with a scattering of sultanas or other dried fruit and caster sugar.

Mix 2 eggs, $\frac{3}{4}$ pint milk and some more sugar and strain over the bread.

Leave the bread to absorb all the wet mixture then bake for about half an hour at gas mark 5. Serve with custard.

Pancakes

I have memories of my mum making pancakes on Shrove Tuesday when I was little. We ended up with bits of pancake on our plates but the sheer theatre of the production – the tossing, flipping and retrieving of parts of the pancake – were hilarious and memorable. I firmly believe that no parent with one pan could ever keep up with the demand for more pancakes because they were consumed far more quickly than they were produced. Even now, I remember the smell of the cooking which lingered and the blue/grey smoke haze that infiltrated the house for hours afterwards.

Every country in the world has its own version of pancakes – some leavened with baking powder as in the USA, some with the addition of potato. The pancake is simply a batter (eggs, milk, flour, butter) which is usually cooked on a hot surface. Variations include crepes, waffles, drop scones, Yorkshire pudding, Staffordshire oatcakes.

The batter is cooked very thinly and flipped to cook the underside. It is usually a very thin cake although this varies according to location. Norfolk pancakes are very thick and cooked in lots of butter.

Shrove Tuesday was the last opportunity to use up eggs and fats before the Lenten fast which lasted until Easter.

My memory of pancakes (once they were safely on the plate) were the toppings. Each household seems to have their own favourite addition to the pancake. It our house, it was always sugar and lemon juice then rolled up and eaten with a knife and fork. Other families enjoyed orange juice, apple sauce, ice cream or golden syrup.

Cakes and Biscuits

For many people, powerful feelings and memories are associated with the making of and eating of sweet treats. Whether it is the association of the person making the cake or biscuit, or the comforting sweetness of the food itself, or taking part in the process, positive memories are cemented. Cakes and biscuits are often shared in times of celebration (Christmas, birthdays, weddings) and family gatherings.

For me, my mother did not have time to bake, so she asked an elderly neighbour to show me how. I remember everything about the first thing I made with her. Melting Moment biscuits. They have never tasted so good since.

Rolled Vanilla Cookies

"3 $\frac{1}{2}$ cups flour
1 tsp baking powder
$\frac{1}{2}$ tsp salt
1 cup shortening (butter or margarine)
1 $\frac{1}{2}$ cups sugar
2 eggs well beaten
1 $\frac{1}{2}$ tsp vanilla
Coloured decorating sugar (optional)

In the first bowl:

Sift flour. Add baking powder and salt. Sift again.

In the second bowl:

Cream the shortening. Gradually add sugar and continue to beat until light. Add well-beaten eggs and blend thoroughly. Add vanilla.

Combine dry ingredients and creamed mixture. Mix all thoroughly and chill for half an hour or longer.

Grease baking sheets.

Roll the dough as thin as possible on a lightly floured board and cut with a cookie cutter. Place cookies on the greased baking sheet. Top with coloured decorating sugar, if desired. Bake in hot oven (400 degrees f) for 6-10 minutes. Grease baking pans before each use.

Makes about 6 dozen thin cookies.

These cookies have been a holiday tradition in our family for four generations. The fun is having everyone take a hand in making and decorating the cookies. The children in particular enjoy choosing the shapes and decorating the cookies. We use a variety of cookie cutters which we add to over time. The oldest ones are over 60 years old and feature along with the newer ones when we make holiday cookies, bringing back fond memories. Family and friends who have moved away still ask that we send them these cookies, so they are mailed in the country and overseas when the holidays are here."

(Mary Ann Chang)

Gran's Shortbread

"6oz butter
6oz sugar (preferably caster)
1lb flour – Gran used ½ cornflour and flour
A little water
Caster sugar to dust

Rub butter and sugar into flour until it looks like crumbs.

Add a little water, enough to bring it together into a dough.

Cut into fingers, dust with sugar and prick with a fork to decorate.

Bake for ½ hour in a moderate oven 180 degrees or 160 degrees in a fan oven."

(Amber Peacock)

Mince Pie Cake

"There was always moaning from my dad about how he didn't like mince pies (it never stopped him eating more than his fair share though) so we had mince pies and mince pie cake...which he claimed he did like.

Makes a 20 cm cake.

175g butter

100g light muscovado sugar
3 eggs
225g self-raising flour
300g mincemeat
A healthy pinch of freshly grated nutmeg
A pinch of ground cloves
$\frac{1}{2}$ tsp ground cinnamon
$\frac{1}{2}$ tsp ground ginger
Icing sugar to finish

Line a 20cm cake tin and preheat oven to 190 degrees or 170 degrees if a fan oven.

Cream together butter and sugar until light and fluffy. Gently beat in the eggs one by one and mix through the mincemeat before folding in the flour and spices.

Tip the mixture into the prepared tin and bake for 40 to 50 minutes until golden brown and cooked through. Set aside to cool for 10 minutes before turning out. Sprinkle with icing sugar before serving. Brandy butter is optional but recommended."

(Linden Weaver)

Gingerbread

"At Christmas time, gingerbread is as important to Norwegians as mince pies are to the British.

When my brother and I arrive at my parents' house for the Christmas holiday, we spend half a day making gingerbread. This is one of my favourite traditions. He rolls out the dough and I cut out the shapes while we listen to Christmas music.

In Norwegian, gingerbread is called "pepperkake", which literally translates to pepper cakes. There is no pepper in this recipe, but there is cinnamon, ginger and cloves, which makes the house smell of Christmas.

Many Norwegian families have a tradition of making a gingerbread house in the lead up to Christmas. The parts are glued together with melted sugar, and decorated with icing and sweets. During the holiday, it works as a decoration and keeps the gingerbread smell in the house. When Christmas is over, it is time to smash the pepperkakehus. When we were young, we invited friends over for this occasion. My dad would be the photographer, trying to capture the moment when the children gleefully smashed the house using ladles, spatulas and wooden spoons. Of course, every part of the kitchen got covered in gingerbread.

250g sugar
200ml golden syrup
1 tsp cinnamon
$\frac{1}{2}$ tbsp ground ginger
$\frac{1}{4}$ tbsp ground cloves
250 g butter
1 tbsp bicarbonate of soda
2 eggs

650-800 g plain white flour

1. Put the cold butter in a big bowl and leave to one side. Add sugar and syrup to a small saucepan. Bring it to the boil. Add the cinnamon, ginger and cloves and stir together. Remove from the heat.

Stir the bicarbonate of soda into the syrup mixture. The mixture will now look a bit lighter in colour and expand a little.

Immediately pour the warm syrup mixture into the bowl with the butter. Stir until the butter has melted and the mixture is cold.

Whisk the eggs and stir them into the mixture. Add the flour little by little until you get an even and firm dough.

Put the dough somewhere cold for a couple of hours, ideally overnight.

2. Roll out the dough on a floured work surface and cut out with cookie cutters. Place them carefully on a baking tray lined with baking paper.

Bake at 200-225 degrees for about 8 minutes (depending on the size of the gingerbread.) Let them rest on the baking tray for a couple of minutes before you move them to a wire rack to cool down.

3. If you like you can decorate the gingerbread with icing made of egg whites and icing sugar. Add a drop of vinegar or lemon juice to make the icing shiny.

Gingerbread without icing can be enjoyed with a bit of blue cheese on top."

(Sara Kasperson)

<u>Melting Moments</u>

5oz soft butter or margarine
3oz caster sugar
2tsp vanilla extract or essence
5oz self-raising flour
Oats
Glace cherries

Heat oven to gas 4 and grease two baking trays.

Cream butter or margarine and sugar until very light and fluffy. Stir in vanilla.

Stir in flour and mix well.

Shape a walnut sized ball and roll into the oats.

Place on baking trays and flatten slightly.

Decorate each with $\frac{1}{4}$ glace cherry.

Bake until golden brown but not dark brown (about 10 to 15 minutes).

Allow to cool slightly then lift onto a cooling wire.

These biscuits are so mouth-watering, I doubt if many will find their way into the biscuit tin.

This recipe was shown to me by a kindly neighbour, Mrs Sherriff. My mum did not have time to bake very much as my parents ran a pub. Her kitchen was warm and comfortable with a wooden, farmhouse table in the middle. I also recall all the crocheted blankets and cushion covers around making it very cosy. Mrs Sherriff also showed me how to knit and crochet. Despite many attempts to replicate the flavour, I have never managed to get my melting moments to taste as delicious as they did the first time Mrs Sherriff showed me.

Preserves and Sweets

Sweet rationing came into effect in 1942. There was an allowance of seven ounces a week for everyone over five years old. This was the equivalent of just one sweet a day for most products in the Woolworth's range. By the following year, sweets were becoming scarce and even having sufficient coupons was no guarantee that there would be enough sweets in the shops to buy.

As raw materials were in short supply, chocolate manufactures were forced to substitute products and improvise ingredients. For instance, Cadbury Dairy Milk as withdrawn in 1941 when the government banned manufacturers from using fresh milk. In its place there was Ration Chocolate, made with dried skimmed milk powder.

The war may have ended in 1945 but chocolate and sweet rationing didn't. It was to be another long eight years until 5 February 1953 before the 12 ounces a month ration was finally abolished. Sugar itself was not de-rationed until September 1953.

Many people used to take advantage of a glut of fruit or vegetables by preserving them as jams, chutneys and pickles, bottling them in Kilner jars.

The amount of sugar and therefore sweets which you were allowed fluctuated during the war, ranging from 16 ounces a month down to 8 ounces a month.

My mother, who was brought up in Belfast, remembers that when she and her brother and sister ran out of sweets, they used to suck Oxo cubes!

I have fond memories of sitting on the outside step with a saucer of sugar and a stick of rhubarb, chomping the sour, sweet fruit in the sunshine. It seemed like a heavenly treat.

Who doesn't remember the tinkle of the ice cream van as a child? Running to follow the musical chimes and finding the money to pay for the treat before it drove off to the next port of call. Everyone had a favourite, whether it be an oyster delight or a "99" with a flake a wafer or choc ice. Sunny days at home or ice cream eaten at the seaside, this was a treat that embedded itself in our memories for a lifetime.

My husband, Paul, remembers a local ice cream maker called Mazza. His real name was Giuseppe Corrado and he came to Belper initially as a prisoner of war during world war two. Following a brief return to Naples to see his relatives, Mr Corrado settled in Belper in 1948. His ice cream business was at the top of Long Row and as a small boy attending Long Row primary school, Paul remembers calling in for a penny cornet or a threepenny or sixpenny tub. The shop only sold one flavour of ice cream but Mr or Mrs Corrado and their son, Johnny, would serve customers at a little counter, often dipping the cornet in chocolate bits at no extra charge. He had a van and would tour the Belper area and as far as Matlock, Winster and Darley Dale. You could take a bowl or container into the shop and have it filled with ice cream. Many of their former customers have said that it was the best ice cream they ever tasted and it was a big loss to the area when the business closed. The recipe was a closely guarded secret and local rumour stated that it would only be sold to another Italian ice cream family. This did not take place and Belper has now lost the delicious white ice cream that so many people remember.

Granny Hills' Marmalade

"I remember my grandpa always having this for his breakfast, as did my father and now I do. And I remember my granny and my mother steaming the house up every spring boiling the oranges.

I do it now and it's like a promise for the year to come. The Sevilles come in January when the year has turned.

1lb Seville oranges
2lbs loaf or preserving sugar (I use granulated)
1 $\frac{1}{2}$ pints water used for boiling the oranges
Add 2 sweet oranges and 2 lemons to each 5lbs Sevilles. I do 2+2 to 4 lbs Sevilles nowadays.

Brush and wash the oranges well.

Boil them until the rind can be easily pierced with the head of a pin. Put in cold water.

Put sugar and water to soak in a pan, boil gently for about half an hour until it becomes a syrup. Skim and let it get really cold before adding the cut rind.

Halve the oranges, squeeze on a lemon squeezer and cut up the peel. Then add to the syrup plus the juice and boil gently for 1 hour, stirring often or longer until it jellies.

Put some on a cold saucer from the fridge to test.

No mention of pips which I immediately discard when I cut up the oranges. Many people seem to put them in a bag to help it set but I have never done that.

I have made three lots of 4lb oranges making 42 lbs in all."

(Toby Hardwick)

Peppermint Creams

"$\frac{1}{2}$ lb sieved icing sugar
Egg white
Peppermint essence

Beat the egg white until a stiff paste is formed when mixed with icing sugar. Add a few drops of peppermint. Roll out on a sugared board. Cut into rounds and leave for 12 hours."

(Amber Peacock)

Tablet

"Every Scottish child has someone in the family who makes this really well. In my family it was my mum. I used to get a square of tablet to take to school every day until I was 11. Surprisingly, I've still got my own teeth.

You will need:
2lbs granulated sugar
$\frac{1}{4}$ lb butter
1 tin condensed milk
2 tsp vanilla essence
$\frac{1}{4}$ pint milk

Melt butter and sugar. Stir in the milk.

Boil for 10 minutes.

Add condensed milk and boil until a little of the mixture hardens when dropped into cold water. This takes about 20 minutes. Add vanilla and pour into a greased tin.

Mark into squares when almost cold."

(Amber Peacock)

Soft Ice Cream

"Soft ice-cream… good stuff and good memories. Not a recipe, but I would like to share my memories of one of my favourite sweets: soft ice-cream. When I was a child, in the late '60's, early 70's soft ice-cream was the thing to get in the snack bar. I live in the Netherlands and our equivalent of the chippy is a snack bar. You can buy chips there, with all sorts of snacks to go with that, but no battered fish! And, of course, the snack bar will always sell ice-cream. All sorts of ice-cream. And one type is, of course, soft ice-cream. Now my memories of ice-cream all involve my lovely grandad, as I got my preference for it from him. He was besotted with soft ice-cream! I lived in the same street as my grandparents and my grandad would pick me up to go into town quite often. I loved his company, and, apparently he liked mine as well. Now, in town there was a snack bar with a soft ice-cream machine that worked automatically. You would drop your coin in, and then the magic happened... a biscuit tub dropped down into a holder, the holder with the tub lifted automatically and then the ice-cream appeared and ended up in the tub. It never missed! But it was still exciting...The holder came down again and you could pick up your ice-cream. Pure magic! Now I discovered very soon that if I asked my grandad for an ice-cream, I wouldn't get one! But as long as I didn't ask, we would always get one, as my grandad loved them so much as well. I learned very quickly not to ask... We didn't necessarily have to go into town for it. Only a couple of yards from my grandparents' house was a snack bar as well. It was called "Frites corner" and was run by a family who had fled from Belgium during the First World War. They had the BEST soft ice-cream going! So quite often when I was at my grandparents' house (and I was there very often, I had lovely grandparents) my granddad would say: "go on, get some ice-creams". I was probably six years old, or maybe even 5 when this was already a regular thing. So, I would get some money, went to the snack bar, asked for 4 soft ice-creams, and handed over the money. The ice-cream tubs came out, were all filled with soft ice, put on a rectangular cardboard plate and wrapped in greaseproof paper. Then back to my grandparents' place, carefully but also as quickly as I could and we would sit there and eat the ice-creams. And depending on if my mum had turned up, we had one extra to share between the three of us. But I never had to go out to buy three, always four. Needless to say I still love soft ice-cream. It is really nice to eat, but there are also a lot of happy memories involved. The taste of soft ice-cream has changed over the years, but sometimes, just sometimes I find the same ice-cream they sold at the Frites Corner. That makes me very happy, as that type is still the best!"

(Ellie Wout)

Luscious Lemon Curd

Grated zest and juice 4 large juicy lemons
4 large eggs
12oz (350g) golden caster sugar
8oz (225g) unsalted butter, at room temperature, cut into small lumps
1 level dessertspoon cornflour

Begin by lightly whisking the eggs in a medium-sized saucepan, then add the rest of the ingredients and place the saucepan over a medium heat.

Now whisk continuously using a balloon whisk until the mixture thickens – about 7-8 minutes. Next, lower the heat to its minimum setting and let the curd gently simmer for a further minute, continuing to whisk. After that, remove it from the heat. Now pour the lemon curd into the hot, sterilised jars, filling them as full as possible, cover straightaway with waxed discs, seal while it is still hot and label when it is cold.

It will keep for several weeks, but it must be stored in a cool place.

To sterilise jars, they should be washed in mild soapy water, rinsed and dried and heated in a medium oven for 5 minutes.

Bonfire Toffee

5oz butter
1lb soft brown sugar
2oz black treacle
2oz golden syrup
2 tbsp milk
1 tbsp vinegar

Place all ingredients in a strong pan and boil for 15-20 minutes.

When a piece is dropped into a cup of cold water and goes brittle, it is ready.

Pour onto a well-greased tin and leave to go cold.

Turn out onto a board and attack with a toffee hammer.

My memory of this was of my dad making this on bonfire night. He did not usually cook but on this occasion, he requested the kitchen to himself in order to work his magic. After much rattling of pans, not a little swearing and much more washing up than the recipe warranted, there emerged a pile of dark, sticky toffee shards which never did set hard.

The very memorable part was the flavour. There was an inescapable taste of vinegar which led me to believe he had not measured the correct quantity. However, my brother and I wrapped up a quantity in greaseproof paper and put it in our pockets as we walked to the local Girls' Brigade bonfire. We tucked into the toffee and enjoyed it as though it were Thornton's or Highland toffee. The bonfire also yielded piping hot jacket potatoes that year, cooked in silver paper at the bottom of the fire. Absolutely delicious on a foggy, freezing November night. My brother and I felt very satisfied as we walked home, seeing our frozen breath hang in the fog and feeling the sticky paper in our pockets.

Cinder Toffee

This recipe is so easy to make and yet spectacular to watch and also eat.

4oz golden syrup
2oz caster sugar
2oz butter
$\frac{1}{2}$ tsp vinegar
1 tsp bicarb
2 tbsp water

Lay out a sheet of greaseproof paper.

Heat the butter, syrup, sugar and water in a heavy-bottomed pan.

Boil without stirring until a spoonful of the mixture becomes a hard ball when dropped into cold water.

Quickly add the vinegar and bicarb to the mixture. It will bubble up.

Immediately pour onto the greaseproof paper and leave for 15-20 minutes until soft enough to score into pieces.

When completely set, break into pieces.

My memory of making this was for my children. Their faces lit up and their eyes widened as the "magic" bubbling occurred like lava flowing out of a volcano. The only difficult thing was to stop them putting in a finger to taste when it was still hot! This is also my dad's favourite sweet or "tutoo" or "tuffee".

For our family, Sunday night was "tutoo" night. After a bath and hair wash, mum used to bring us all in front of the fire to clean our ears, trim our nails and dry our hair. I remember having pyjamas, slippers and dressing gowns on as well as wearing a "turban". Mum used to twist a towel over our heads and throw it over our backs and we would balance the bundle of towel on our heads while waiting for our hair to dry.
While this was going on, dad would go over to Mrs Stewart's corner shop and purchase our favourite sweets. My brother liked flat, brown toasted teacake sweets. Mine were coconut mushrooms. For Dad, it was liquorice allsorts and mum enjoyed (and still does) buttered brazils.

Food Defying Description

Every family has a "meal" which is peculiar to them. It is said that "Necessity is the mother of invention" and this is true where food is concerned. For me, I enjoyed jam and salad cream sandwiches when I was a little girl. My granny used to eat vinegar sandwiches and plenty of people I know enjoyed sugar on bread. And I have heard of bread, sugar and milk when no breakfast cereal was available.

Masterpeas on Toast

"A crusty loaf - white or brown
A can of garden peas
Pat of butter
Apple cider vinegar
Salad cream

Method for one serving:

Pour peas into a pan (in their own juices) and heat on the hob or in a bowl in the microwave until thoroughly cooked through - stir often.

At the same time toast two thick cut slices of bread.

Butter the toast evenly and arrange on a plate.

Lightly sprinkle the buttered toast with apple cider vinegar.

Pour one tablespoon of the pea juice onto each slice of toast.

Using a straining spoon evenly distribute the peas over each slice of toast.

Drizzle salad cream all over the peas.

It is important that the toast and peas are cooked at the same time as this dish is at its best served hot.

A warm plate is recommended.

The phrase "necessity is the mother of all invention" will have been realised by many students when faced with a bare cupboard or fridge. I wanted beans on toast and indeed craved them but there were none to be found in any of the dark recesses of the kitchen regardless of a frantic hunt accompanied by an occasional and exasperated "I'm sure there was a tin here yesterday!" and "There are always bloody cans of beans in here!".

On this particular day, of beans, there were none.

Ah! But there is a can of peas! Peas on toast! Why not? The principle is the same, just replace one thing with another. Ketchup on peas? No. But salad cream might work!

And a little vinegar to spice up the toast too.

Peas on Toast was created and is a pleasant, cheap and filling dish (suitable for both vegetarians and vegans - substitute a different spread for butter) suitable for lunches or tea.

Additions maybe slices of cooked ham and a selection of cheeses with chutney."

(Mike Haynes, Drama Student in Staffordshire circa 1994)

Sore Ear 'Oles

These little tarts are made by using pastry tart cases and filling them with frangipane mixture round the outside of each case. In the centre a few sultanas are sprinkled and finished off with a blob of jam in the middle. When baked, these small tarts have the appearance of "sore ear 'oles" according to Rick's grandad.

(Rick Peacock)

Strange Sandwiches

When I was a small child, I had a penchant for strange sandwiches. My favourite of all time being jam and salad cream together. Grandma Kitty would regularly eat vinegar sandwiches and I have heard many tales of sugar sandwiches.

Who can forget stinky egg sandwiches, especially when taken on school trips and eaten on the bus?

Fish finger sandwiches have now become rather popular and I regularly see them on pub menus, dressed up as "posh".

About "All Around the Shire"

Janet Barrass B.Ed (Hons.) R.N.L.D.

"All Around the Shire" is a self-funding social enterprise that is a celebration of happy memories.

In my career, I have followed a diverse path, training initially as a nurse for people with learning difficulties and then teaching for many years in both special and mainstream schools. In latter years, I have been involved with older adults in the care at home sector. In my own family, it has been my privilege to come from a carer's background and to travel with close relatives on their journey through memory problems.

Paul worked for nearly 40 years in the NHS as a senior occupational therapist, supporting older people and their carers. He specialised in psychiatry and older people's mental health and has extensive experience working with people with different types of dementia. Paul is also a carer for a close relative.

Paul gives training on dementia and how to live well with the condition. He has written several books including one on Friendships and Relationships.

Using our combined knowledge together with our personal and professional experience, we have developed an interactive, therapeutic approach to reminiscence activities.

Our sessions started as "My mum had one of those": a nostalgic look at original artefacts which we collected together for people to remember items which may have once been familiar to them. We put these objects together with snippets of songs, monologues, stories, jokes, poems and quizzes to produce a multi-sensory and gently- paced session for groups. We also use costume to provide visual stimulation and spark memories. Our sessions are responsive, and change according to the memories which are evoked. We understand the different barriers to communication and our sessions can be tailored for specialist groups and individuals.

"All Around the Shire" also delivers themed sessions which focus on memories of "Happy Holidays", "Schooldays", "The Fabulous Fifties", "Wartime Memories", "Historical Hats", "Springtime and Easter Traditions" and "Christmas Traditions".

Our sessions are for everyone. As you will have realised, mealtime memories are something that we all have in common regardless of age, ability and experience.

Most of all, our desire is to see people experiencing enjoyment, participation and living well in spite of the challenges that older age can bring.

If you would like to know more about our groups, we can be contacted by:

Telephone: 07949 371585
E-mail: allaroundtheshire@btinternet.com
www.allaroundtheshire.com